Art Nouveau Coloring Book

30 Coloring Pages for Adults of Alphonse Mucha Illustrations

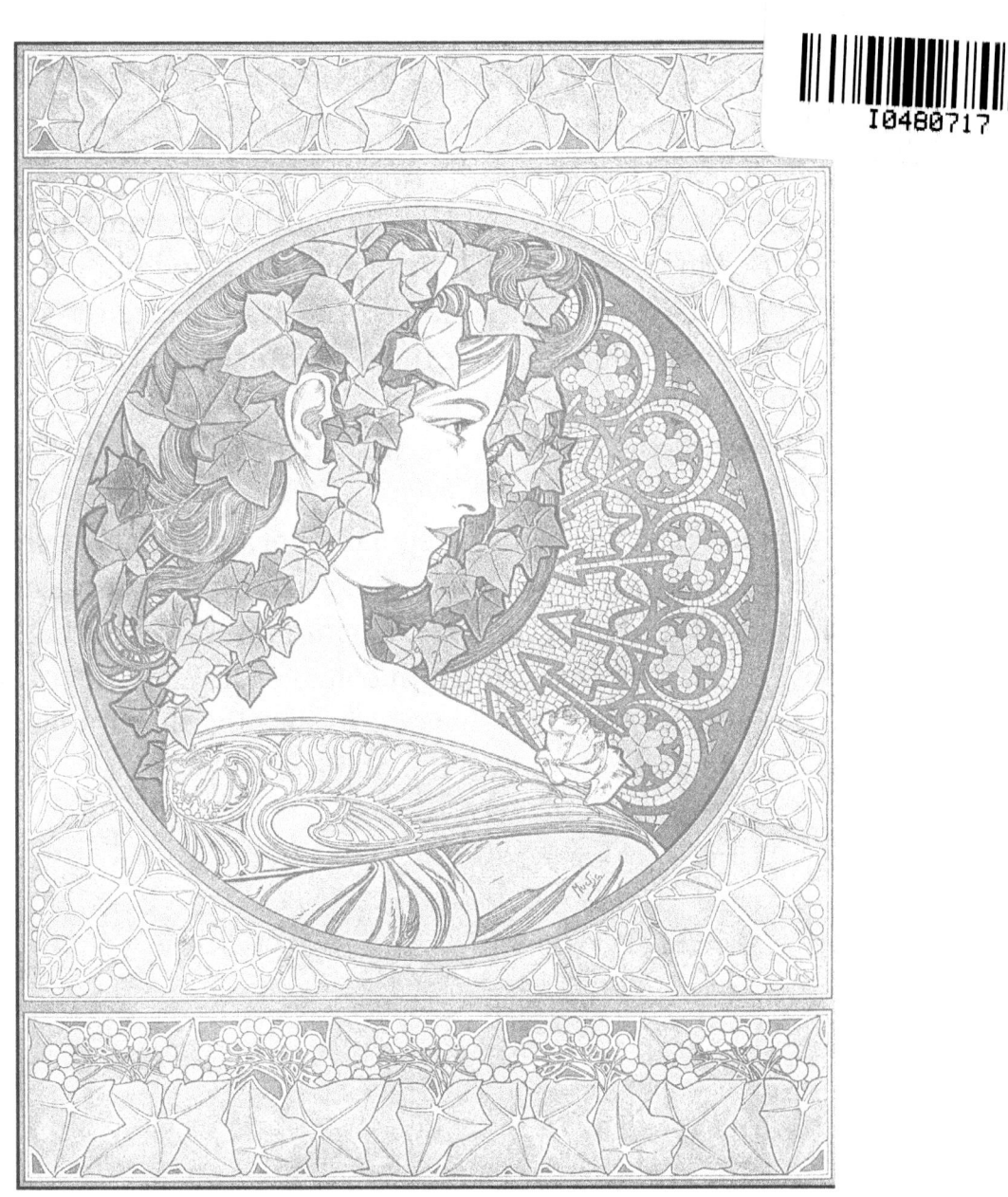

I0480717

Ada Ashley

In this art coloring book, you will find 30 most beautiful art nouveau illustrations from the famous Alphonse Mucha, reproduced true to original in light grayscale, perfect for realistic coloring and art therapy relaxation. Illustrations are reproduced without hard outlines for the opportunity to color them as actual artwork and be proud to cut out and display after finishing. In addition to coloring, this book allows you to practice drawing, shading, and tracing based on the artwork of a master illustrator.

The advantage of grayscale coloring over regular coloring is that the shading is already done, providing the depth and dimension to the final result. It also allows you using the existing shadows for guidance. General rule for grayscale coloring is simply to apply light colors over light gray areas, medium colors over medium gray areas and dark colors over dark gray areas. Alternatively you can start lightly with one color over larger areas and gradually add darker layers on top of it.

Ada Ashley

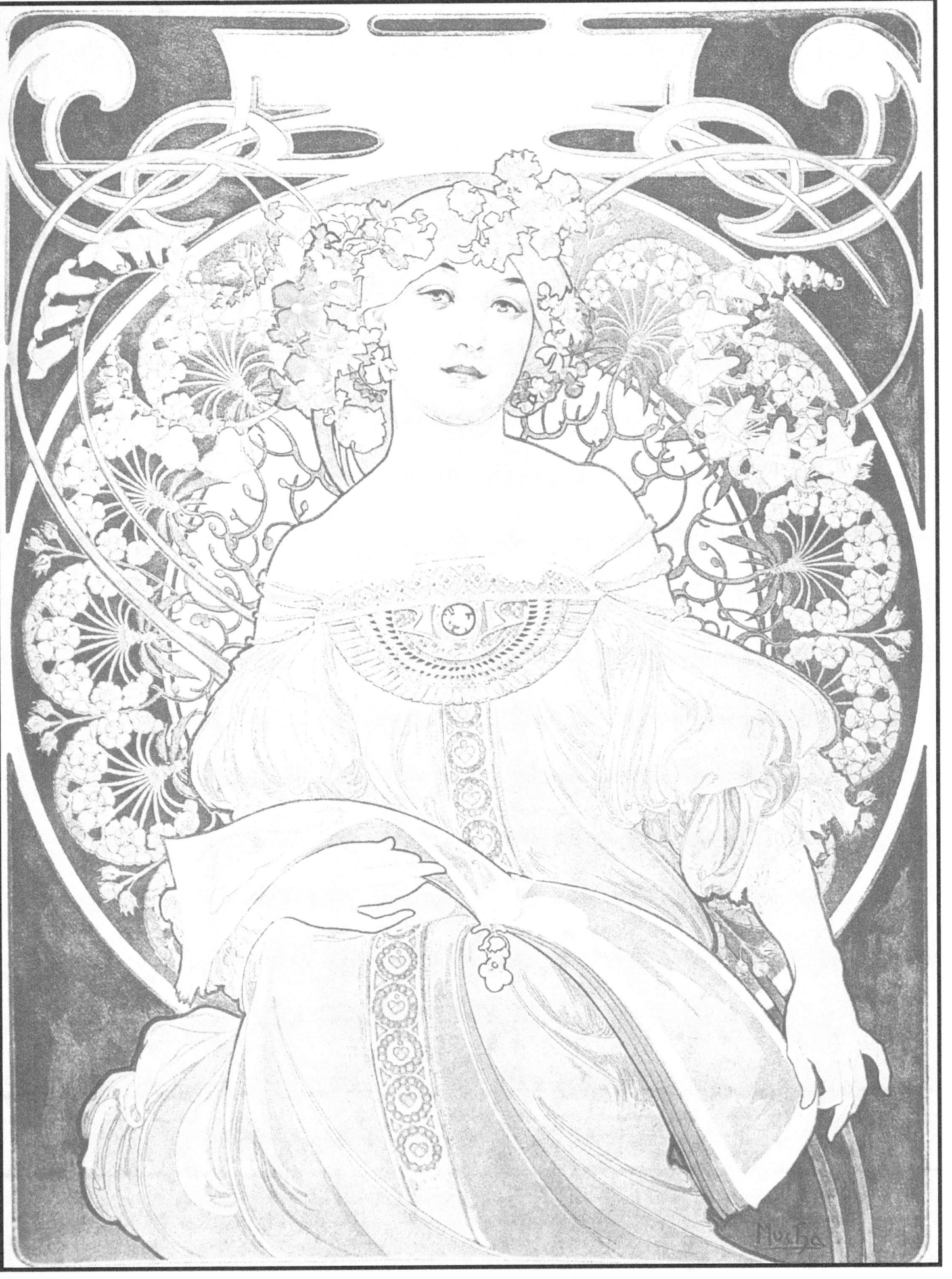

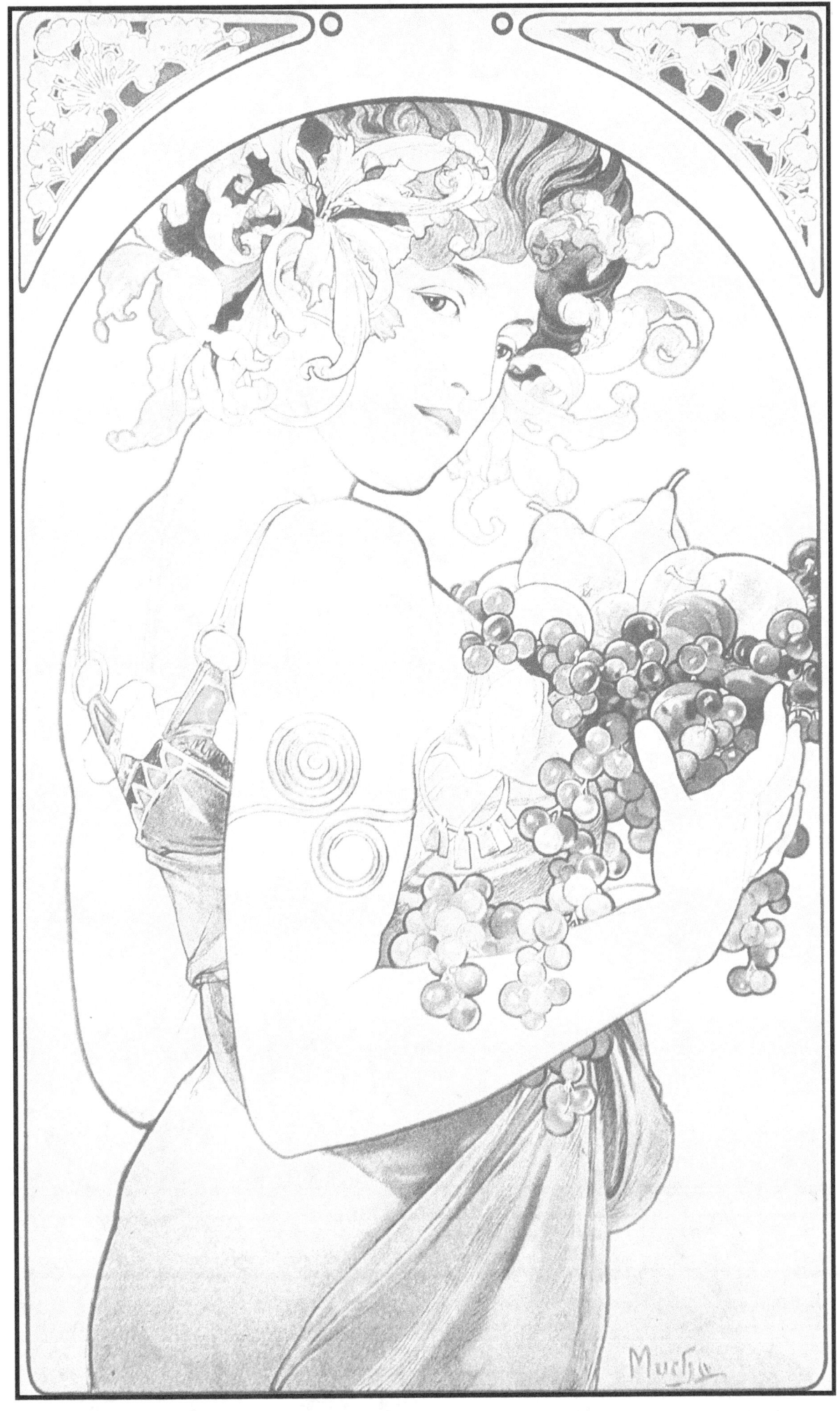

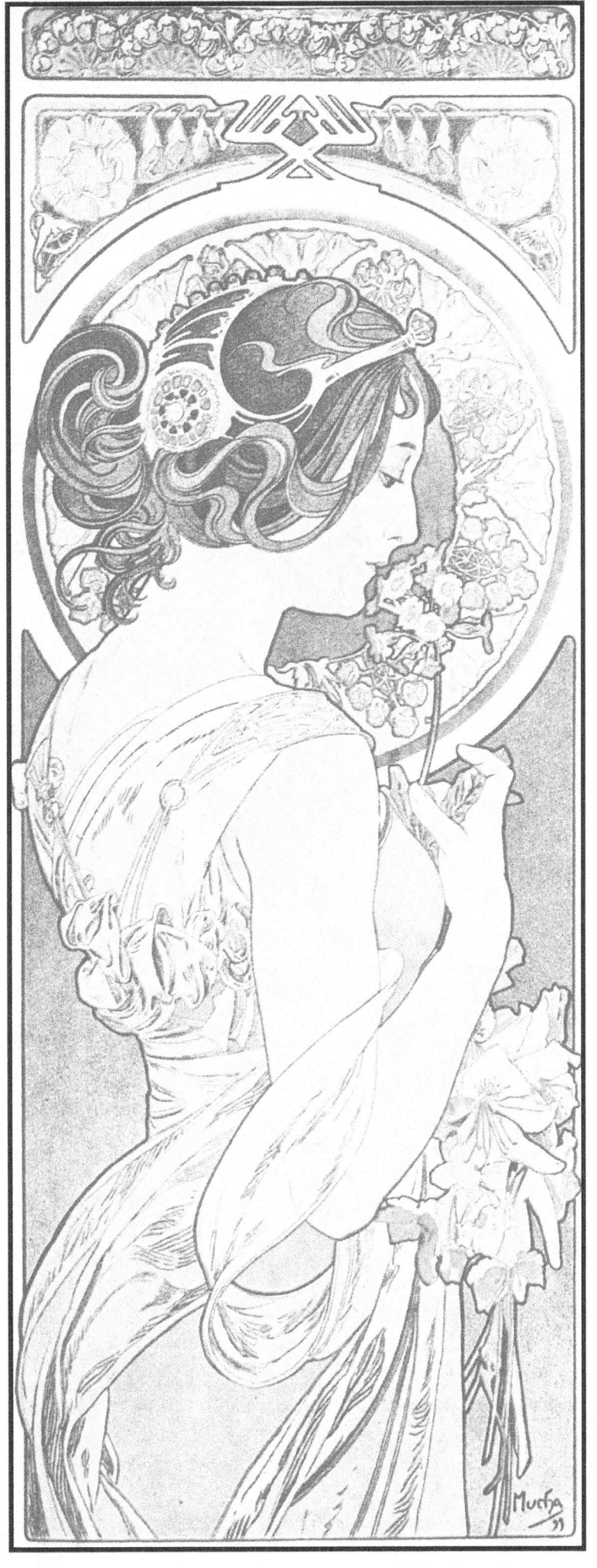

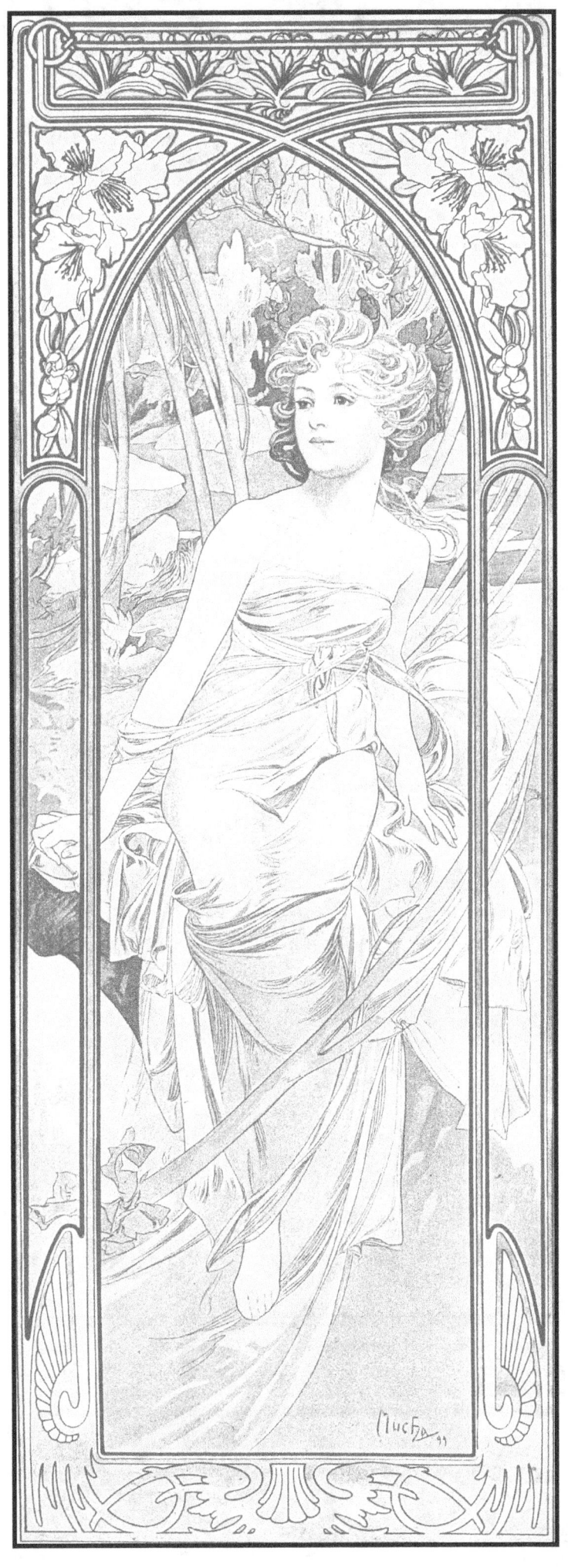

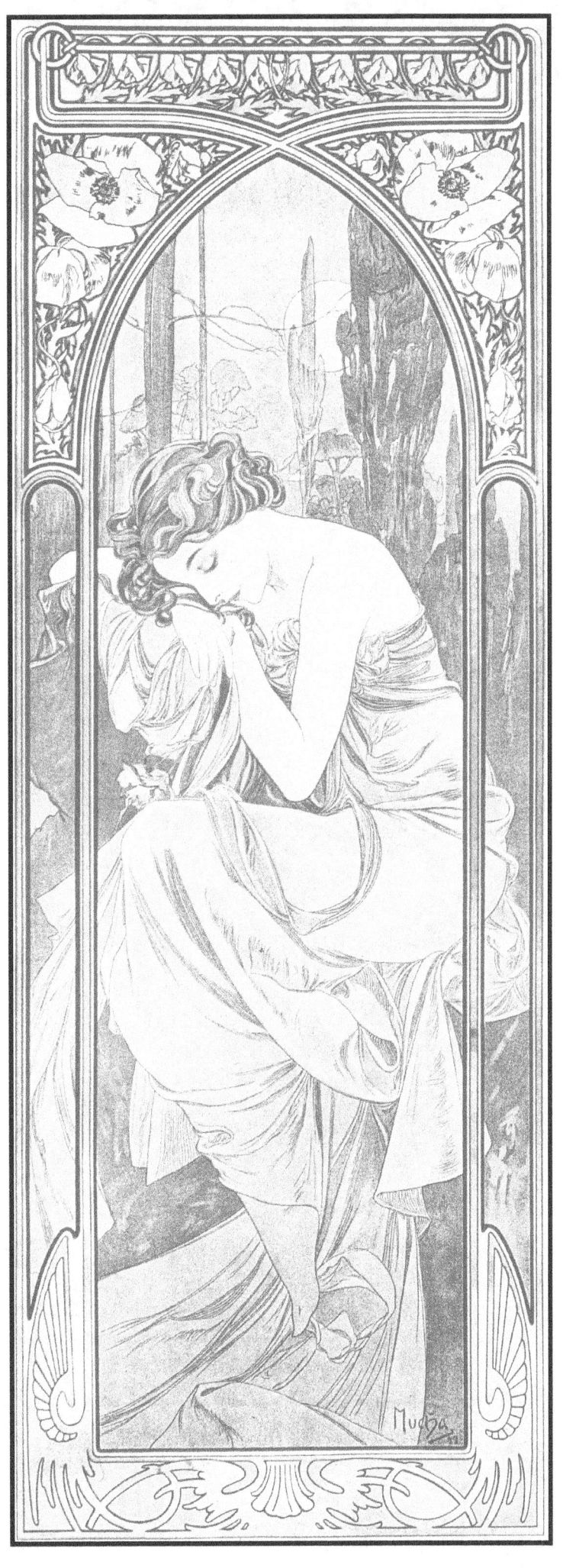

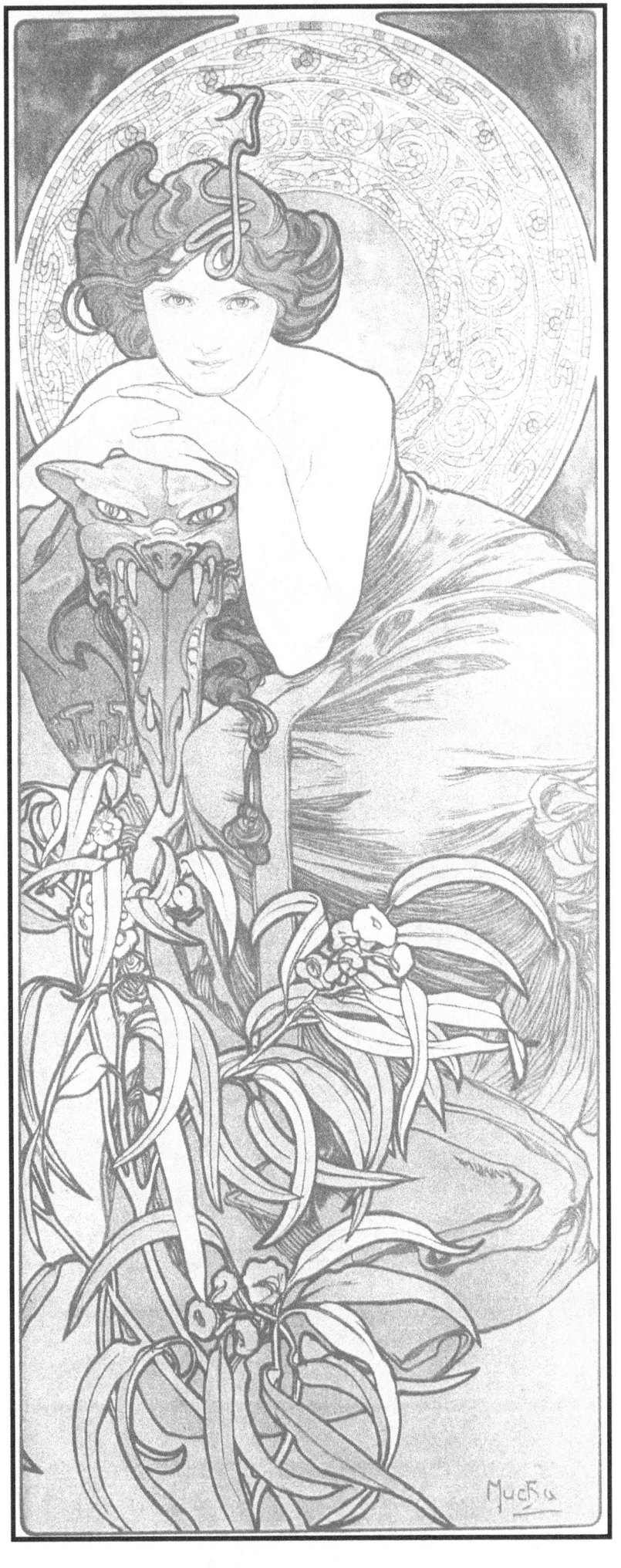

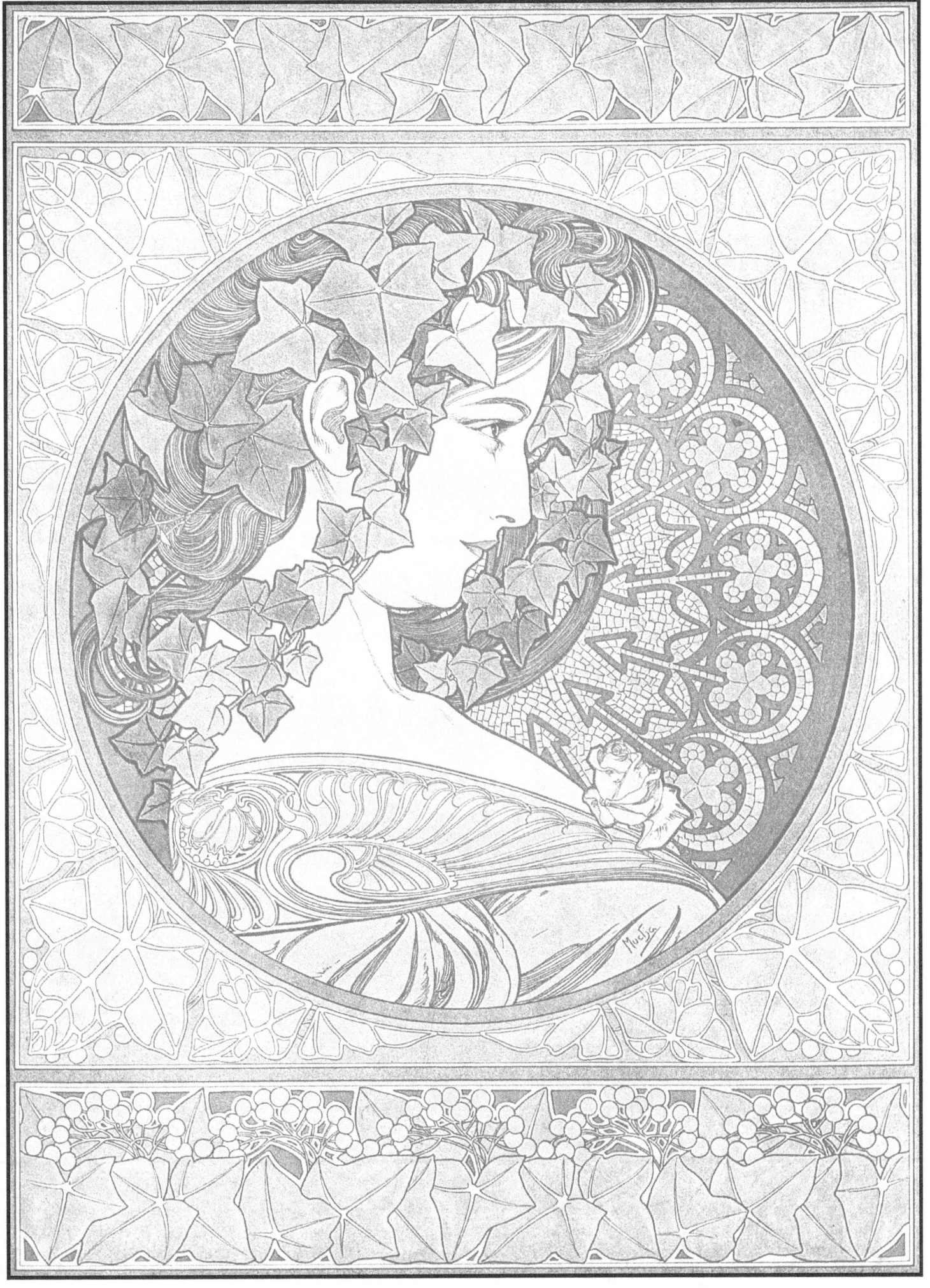

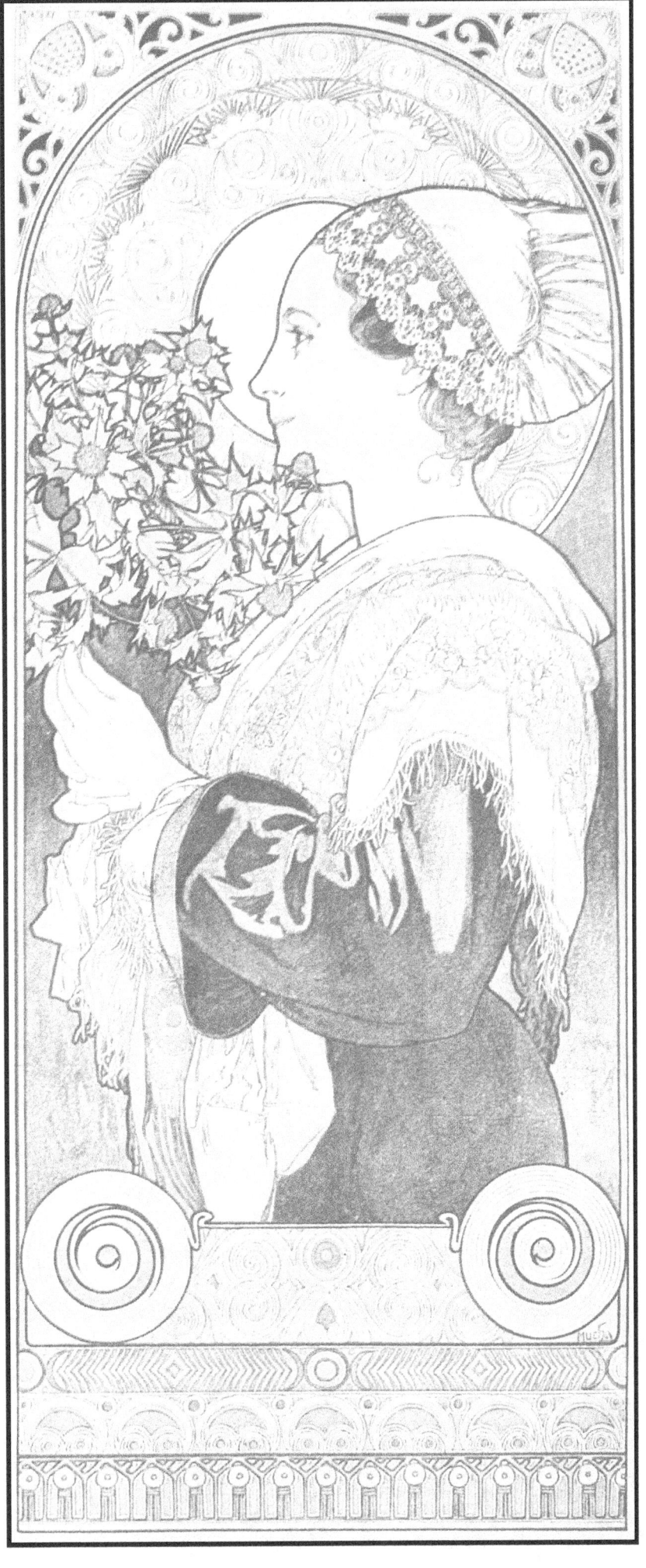

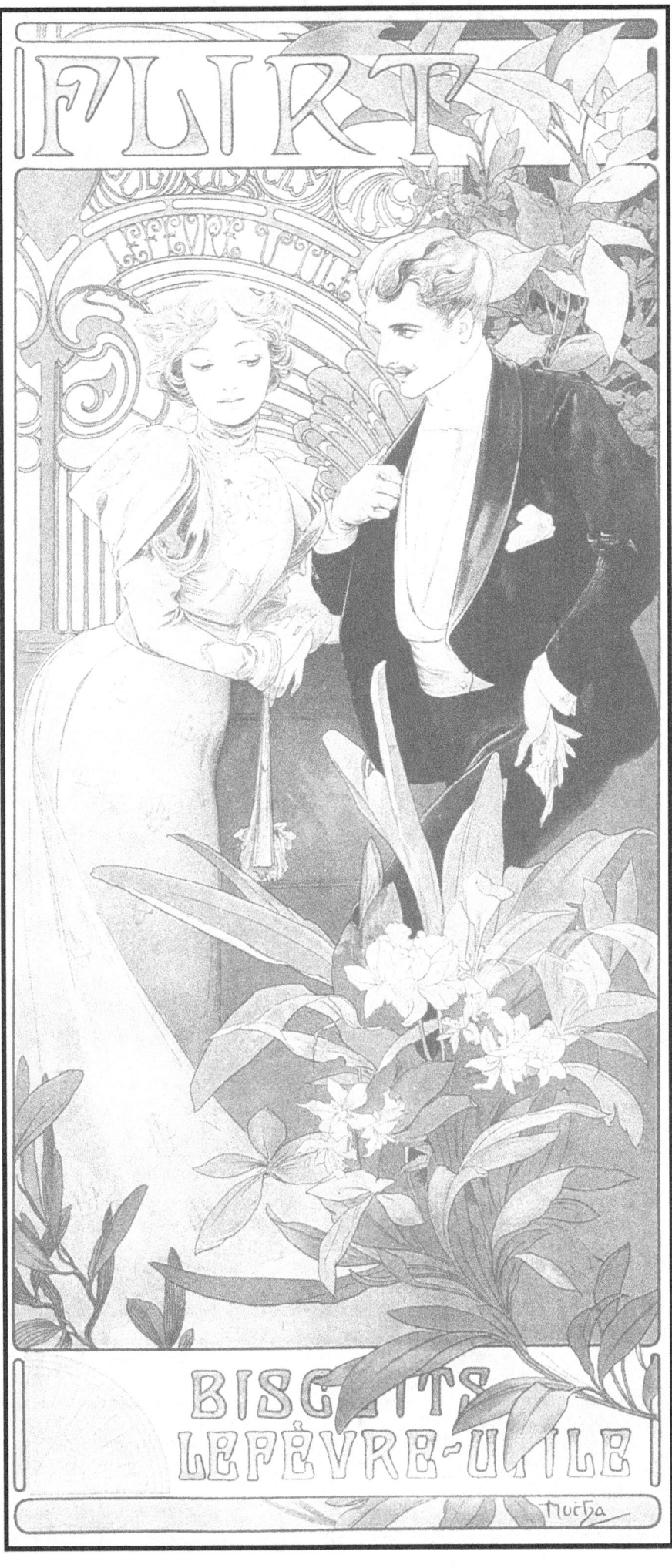

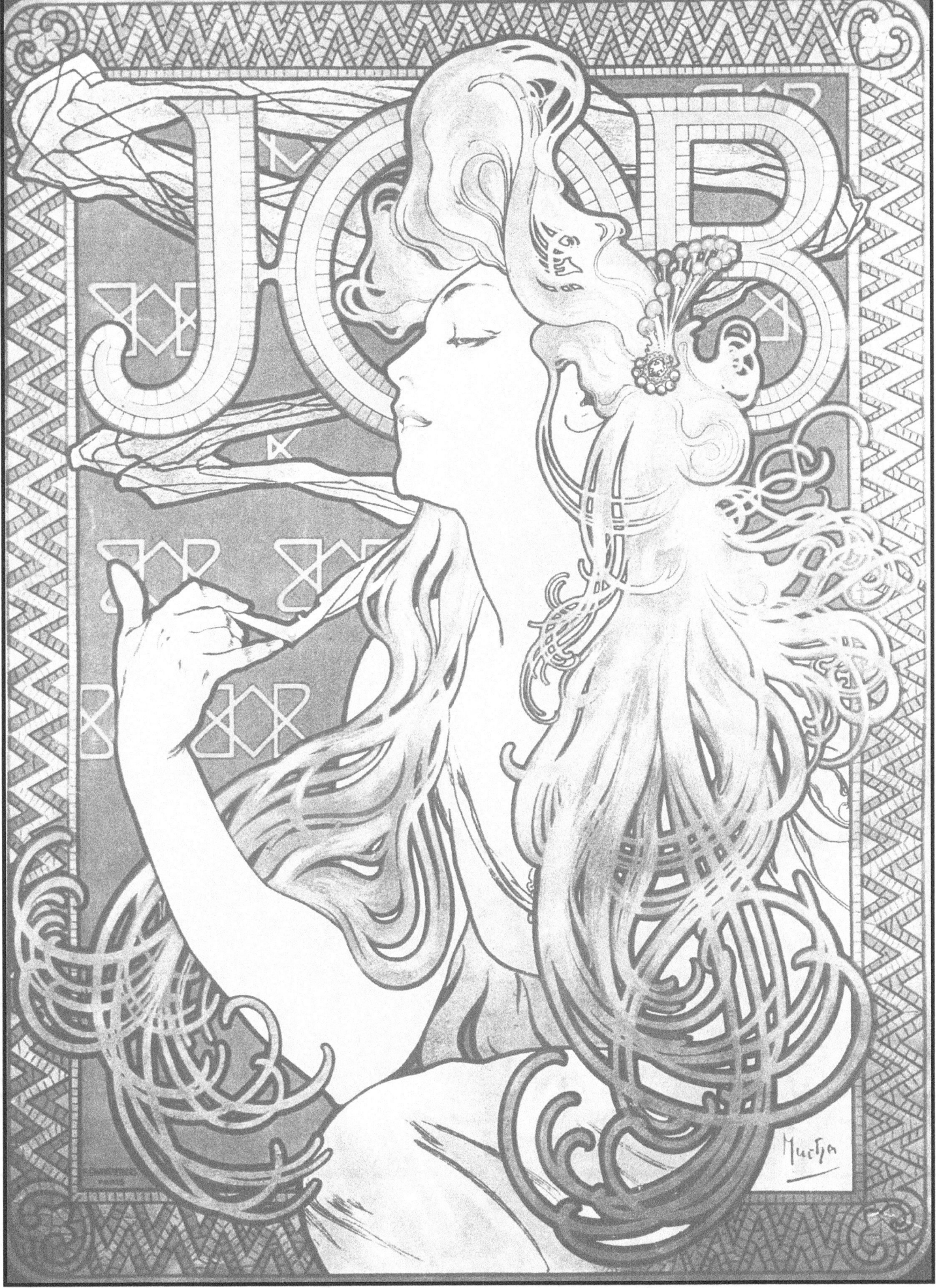

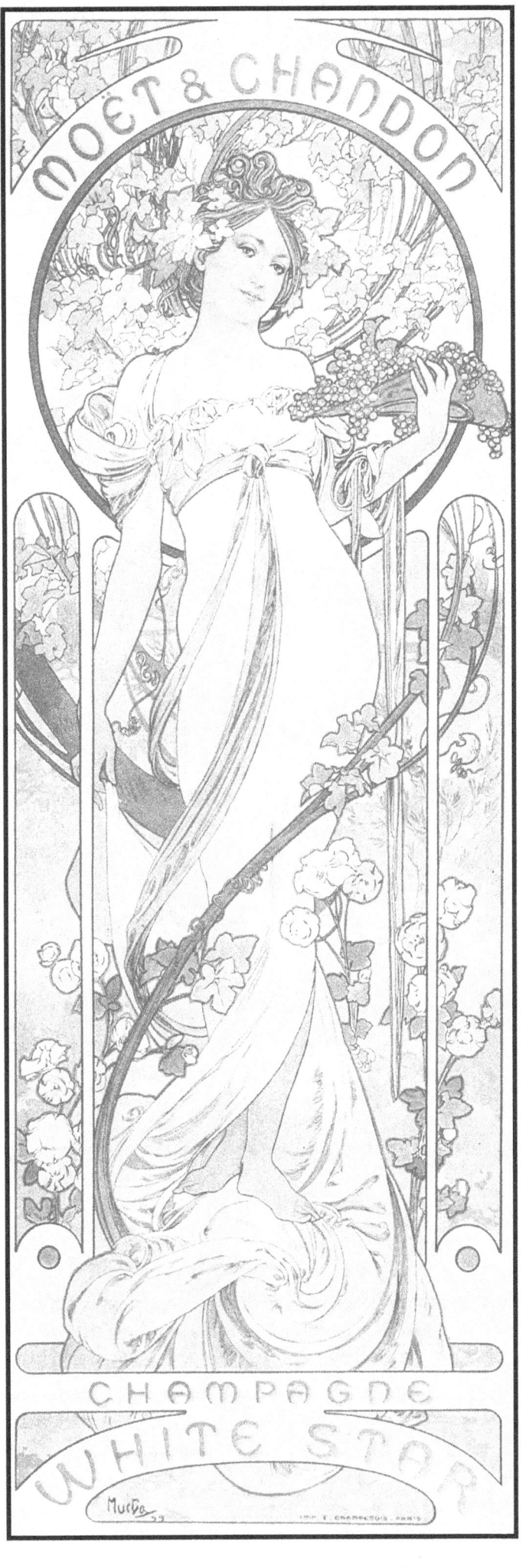

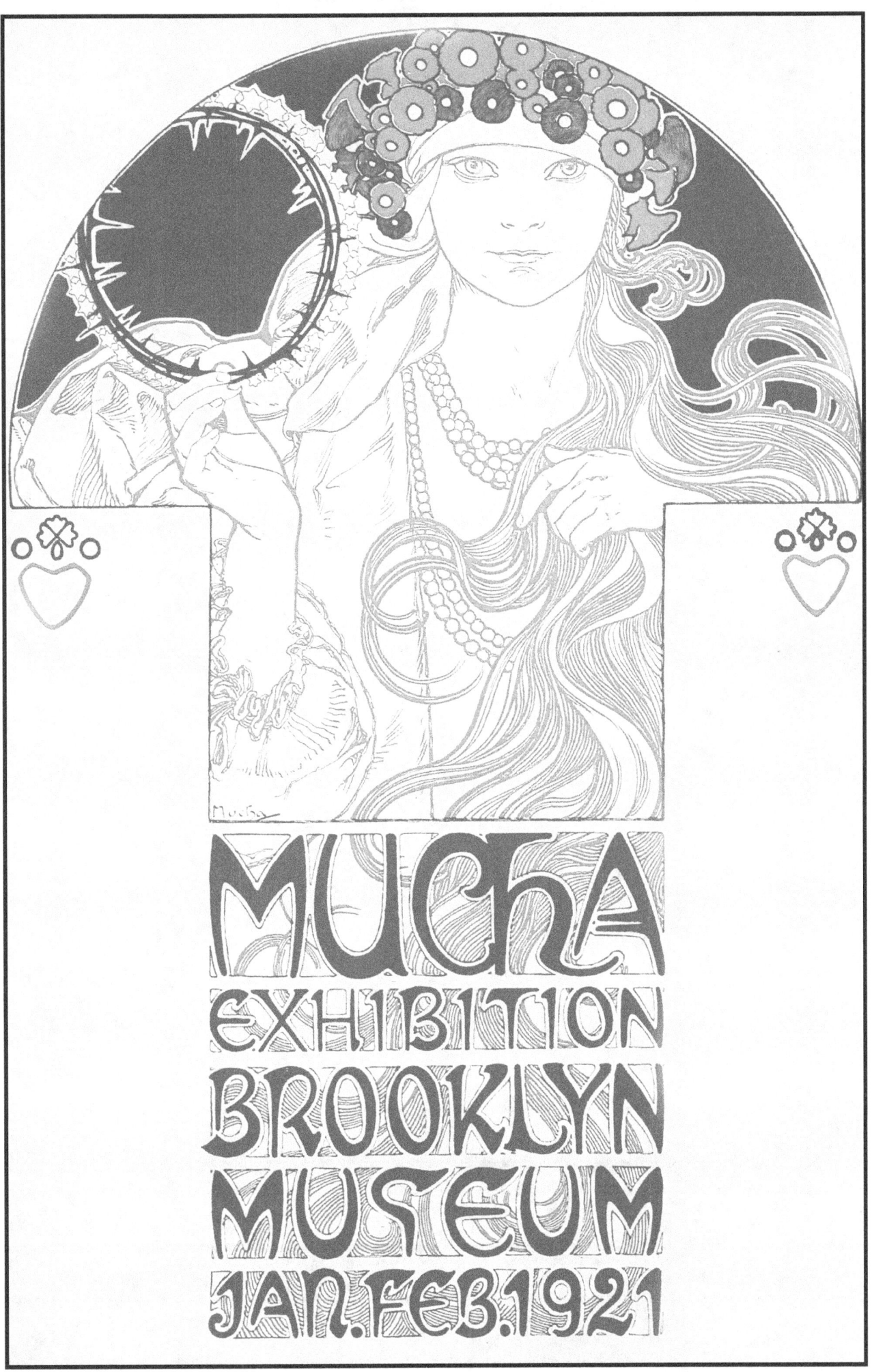

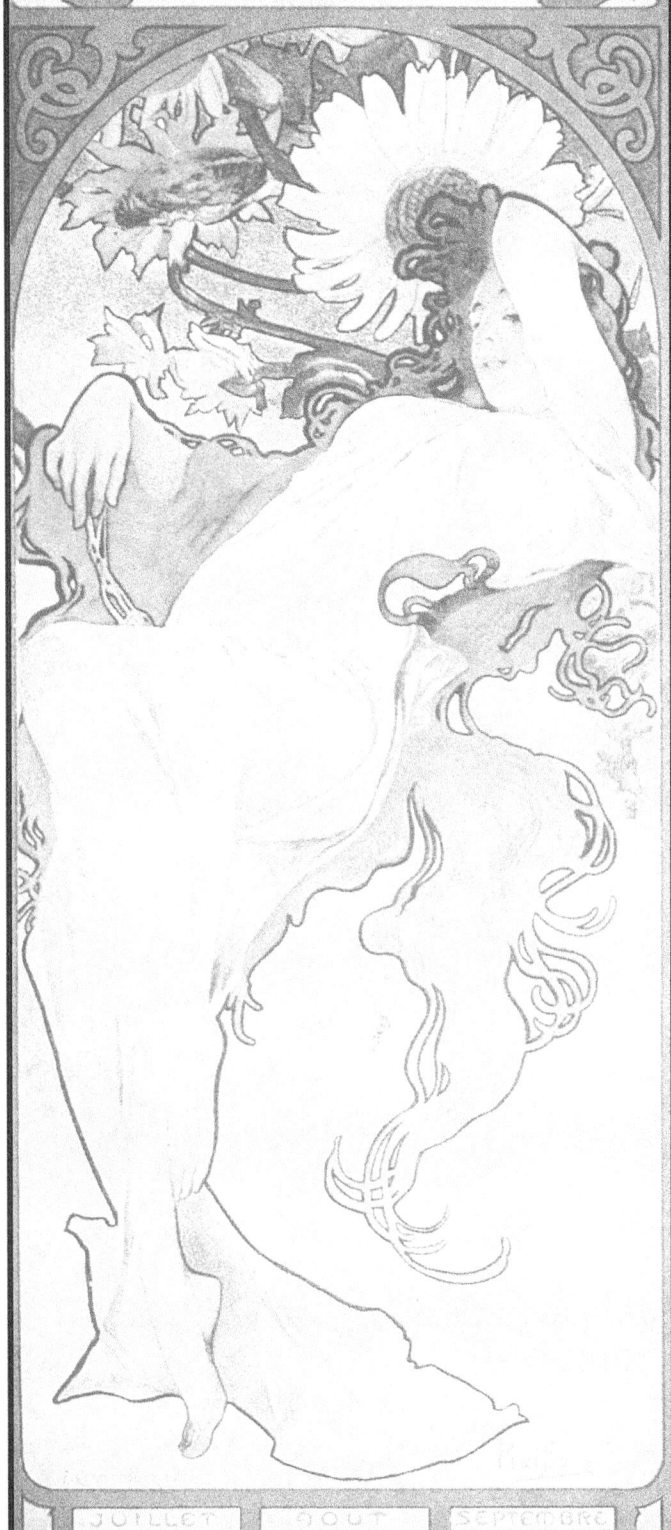

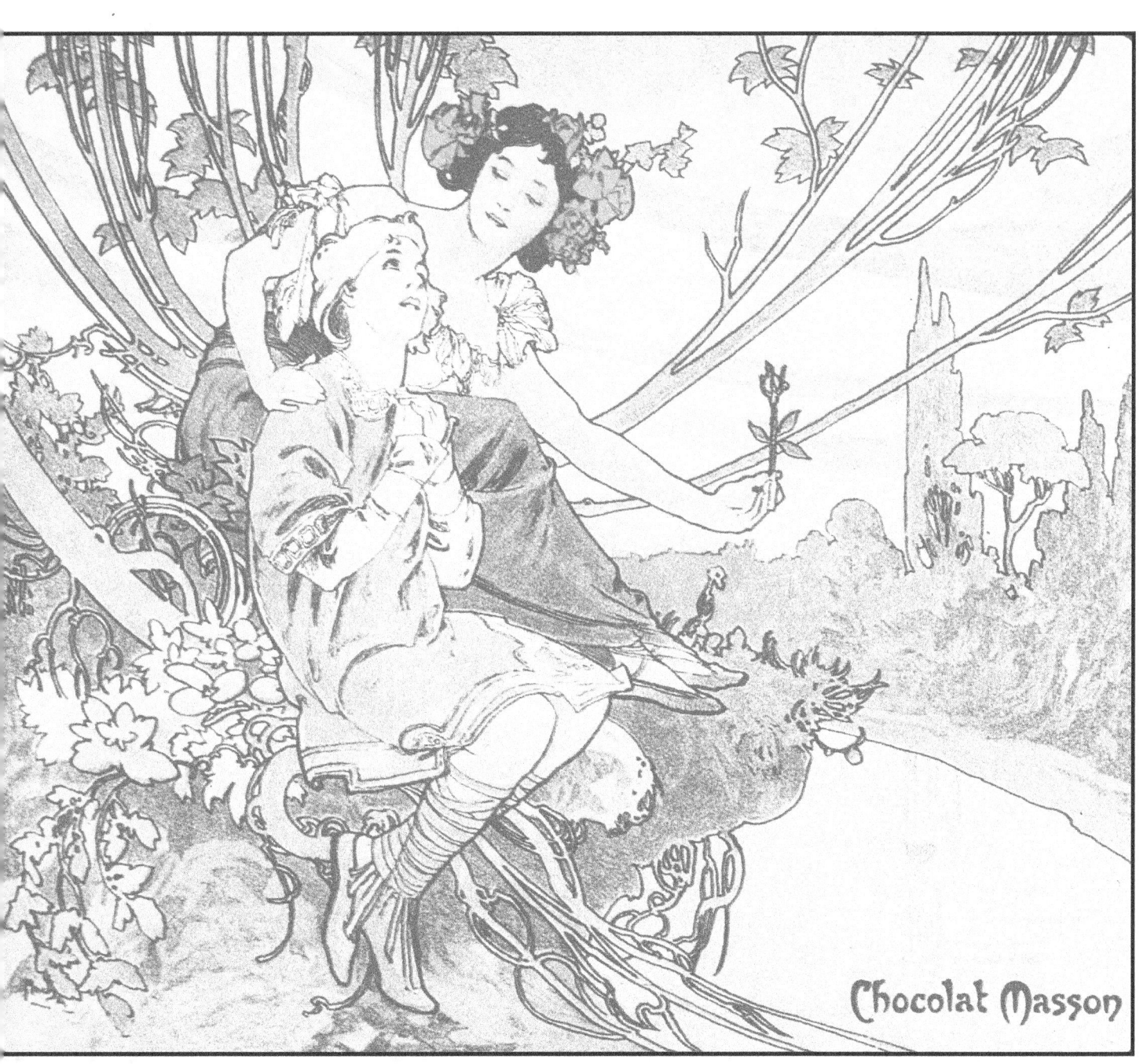

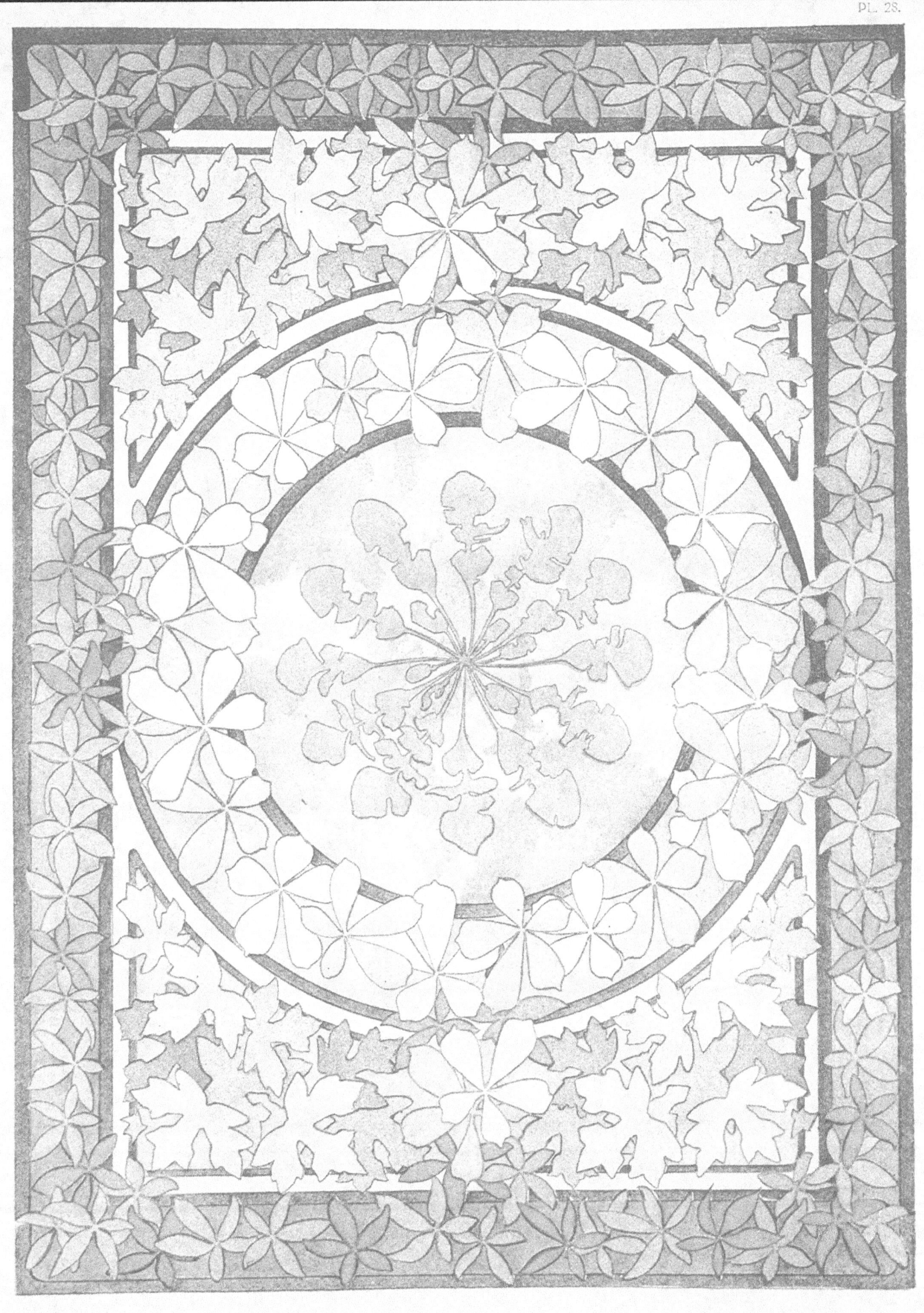

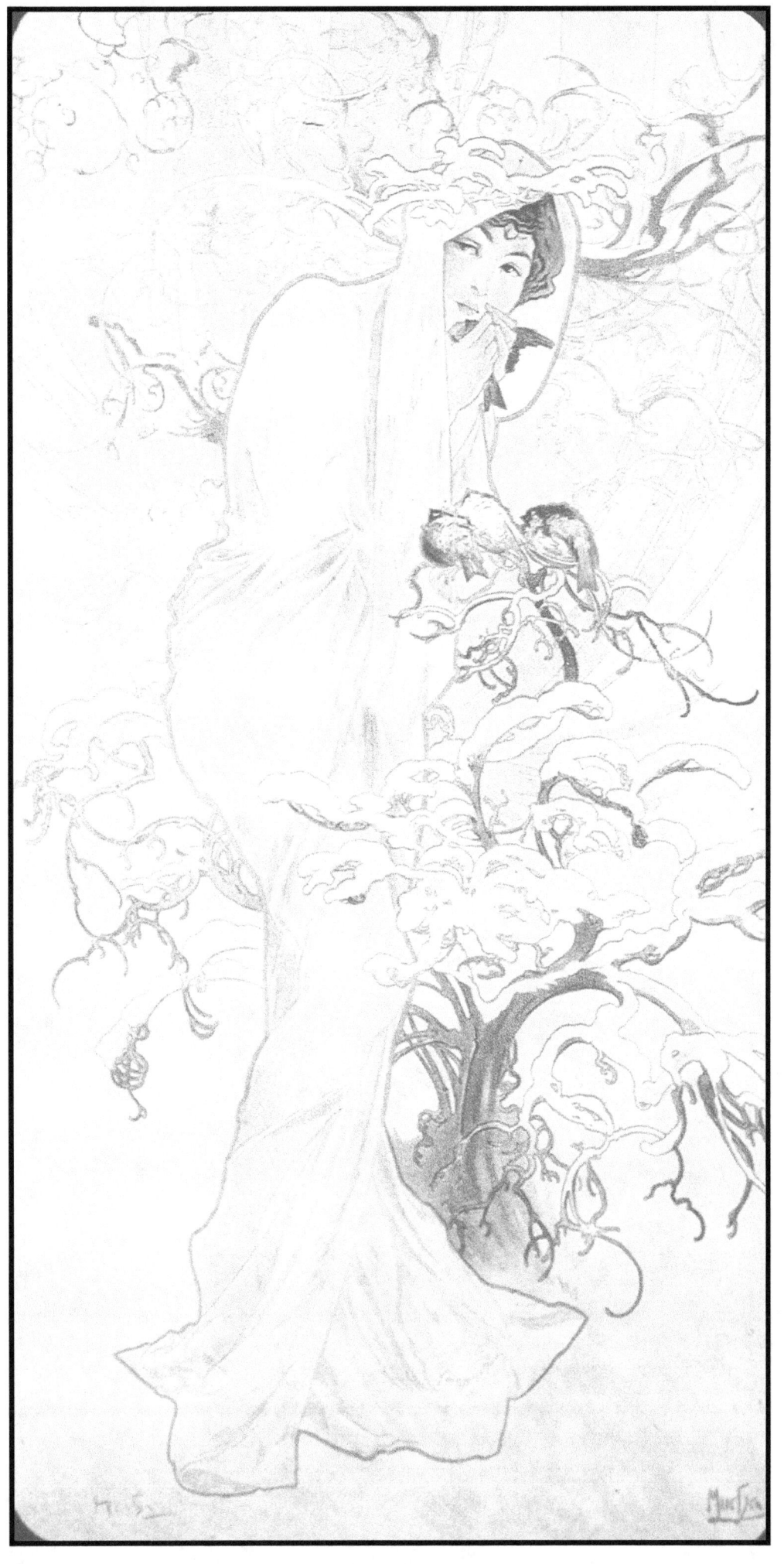

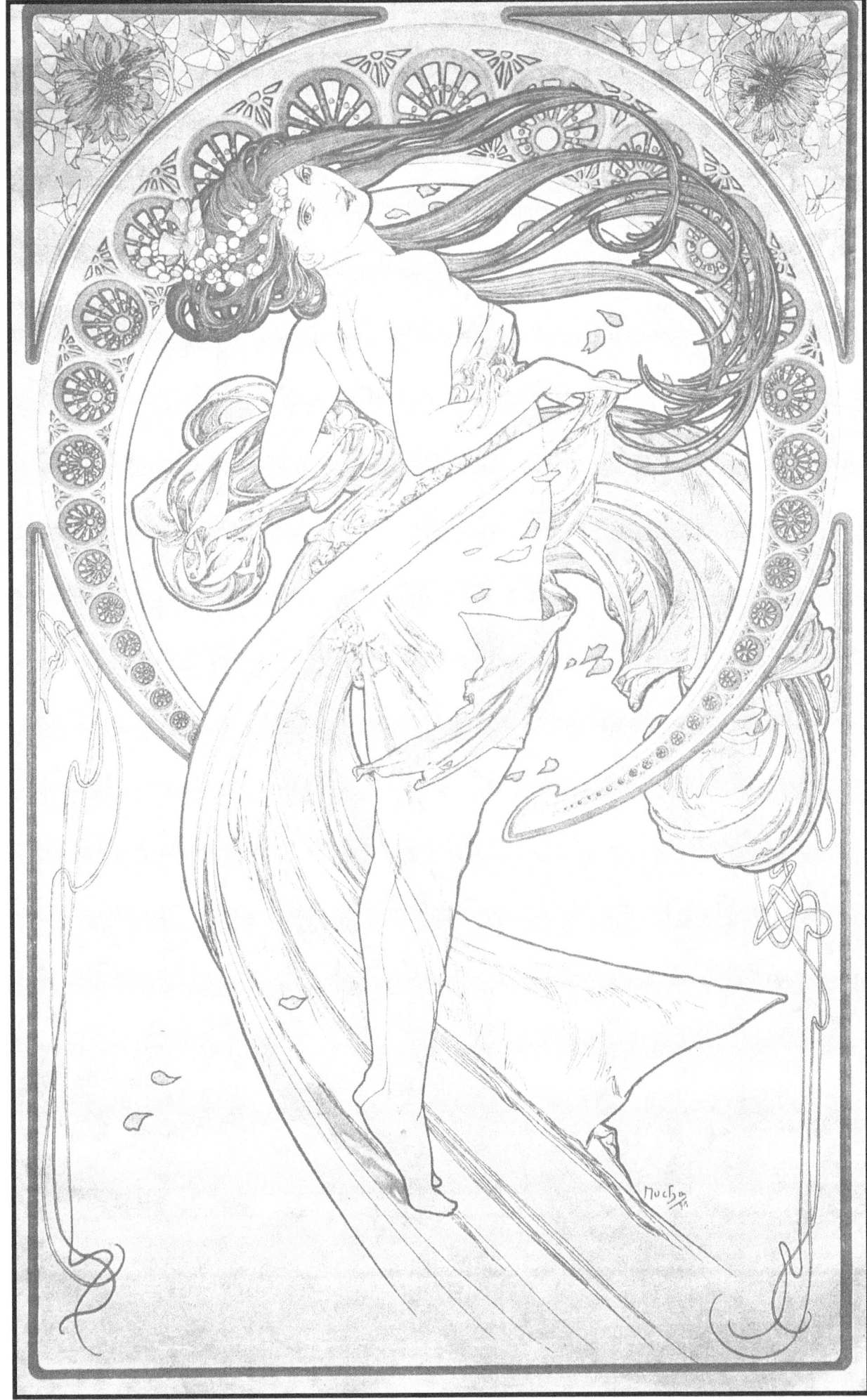

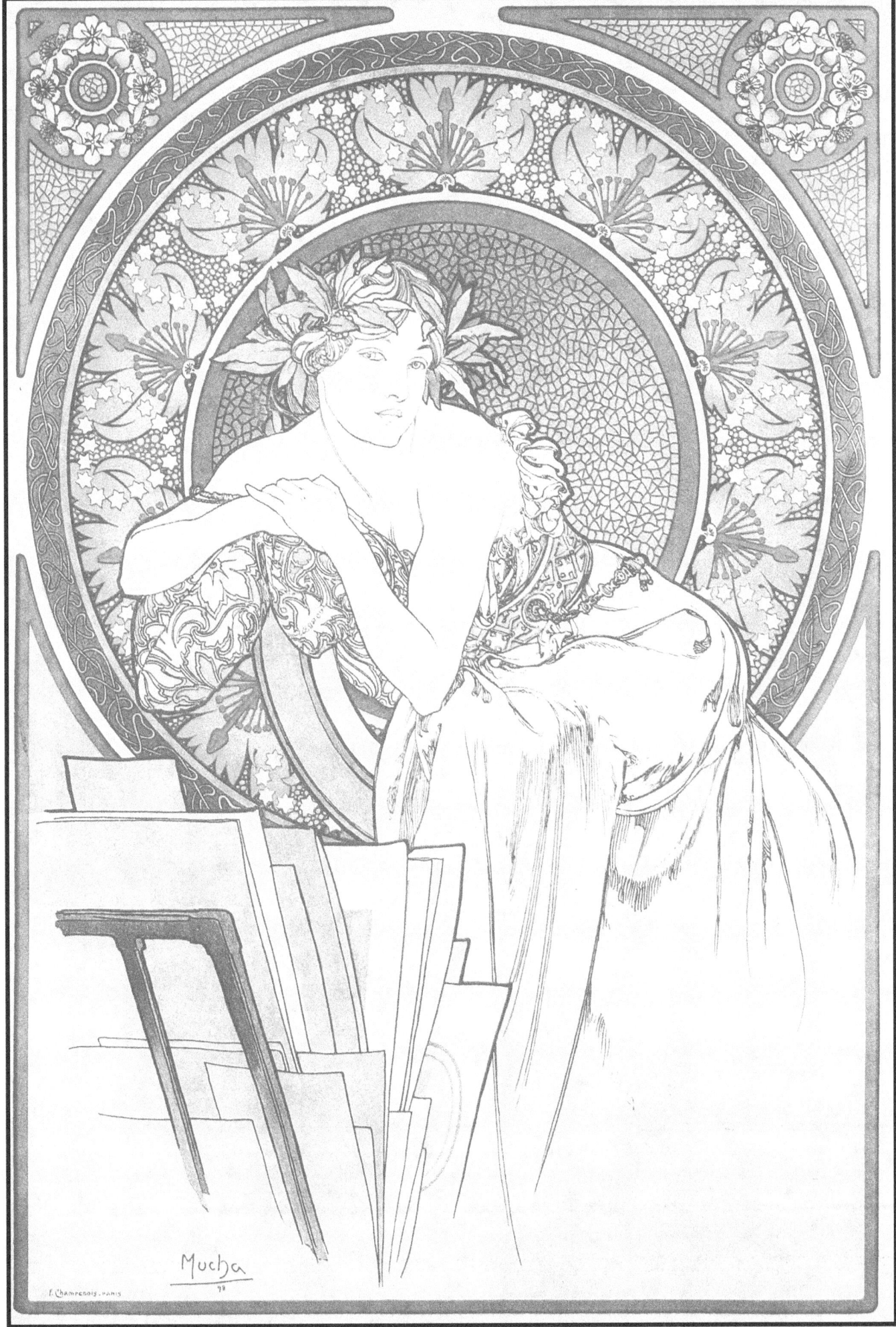

Mucha

F. Champenois. PARIS

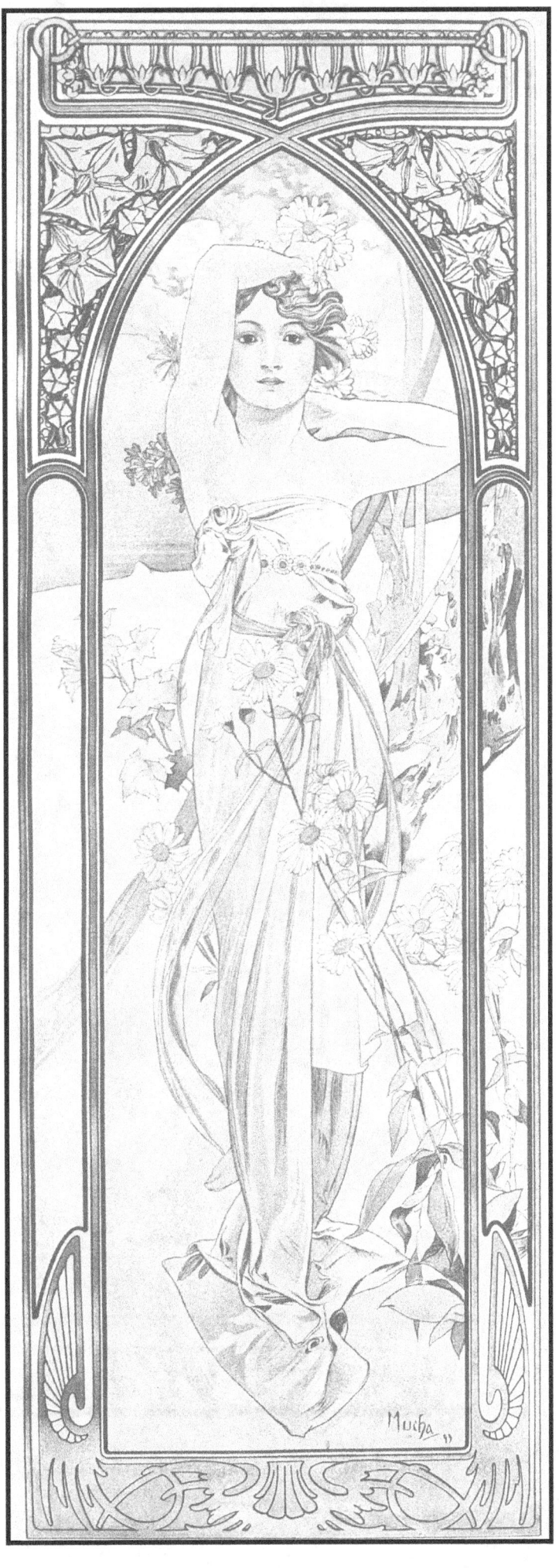

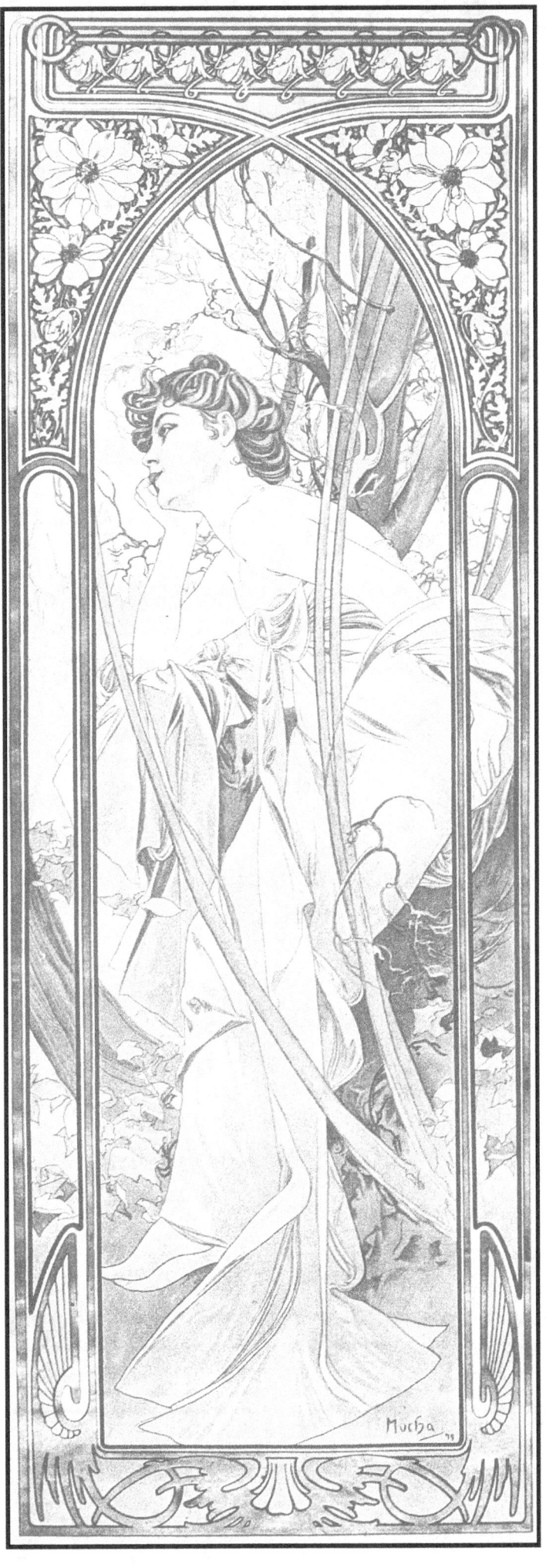

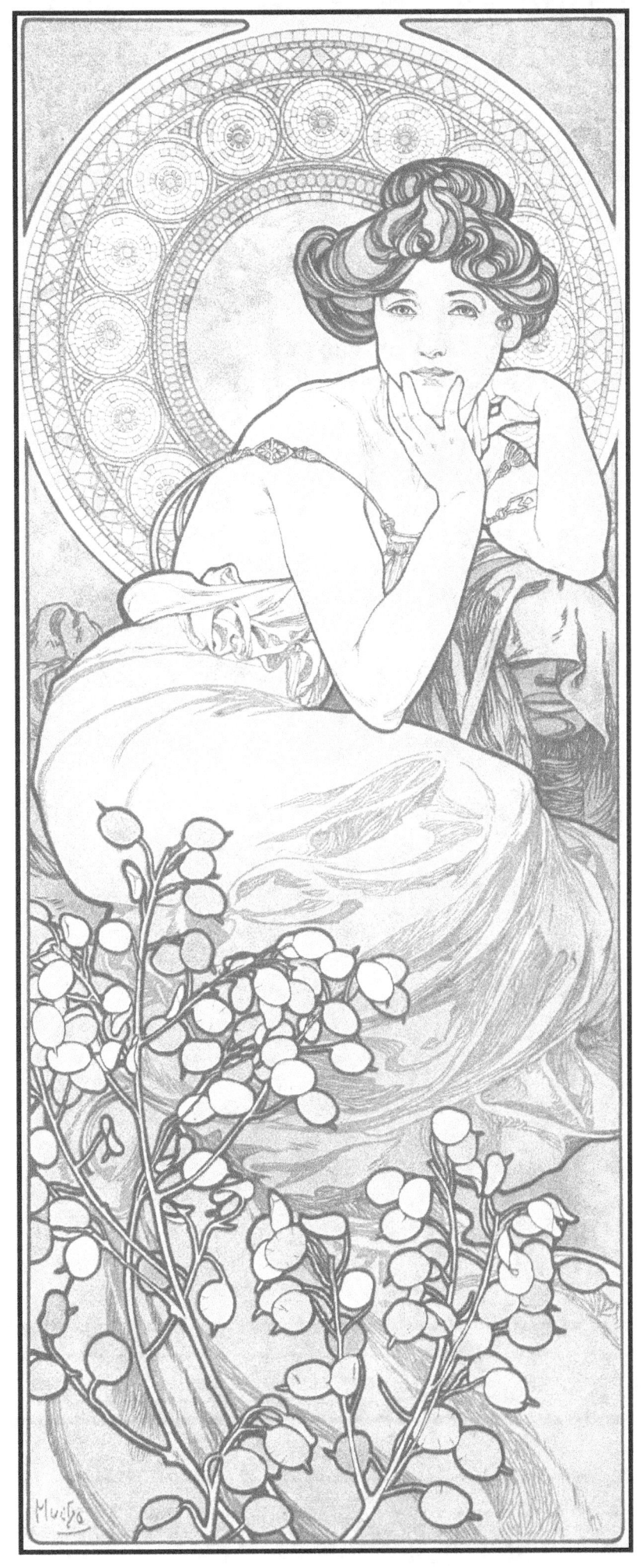

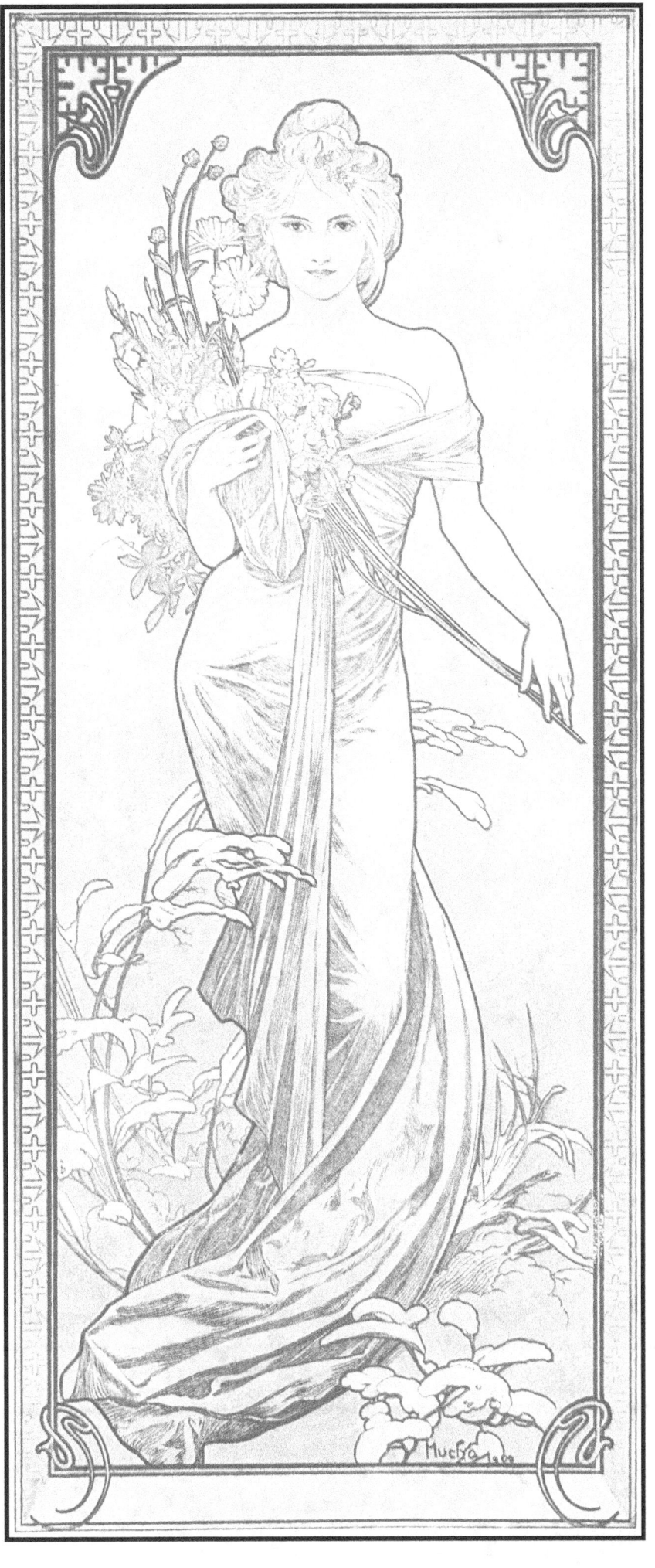

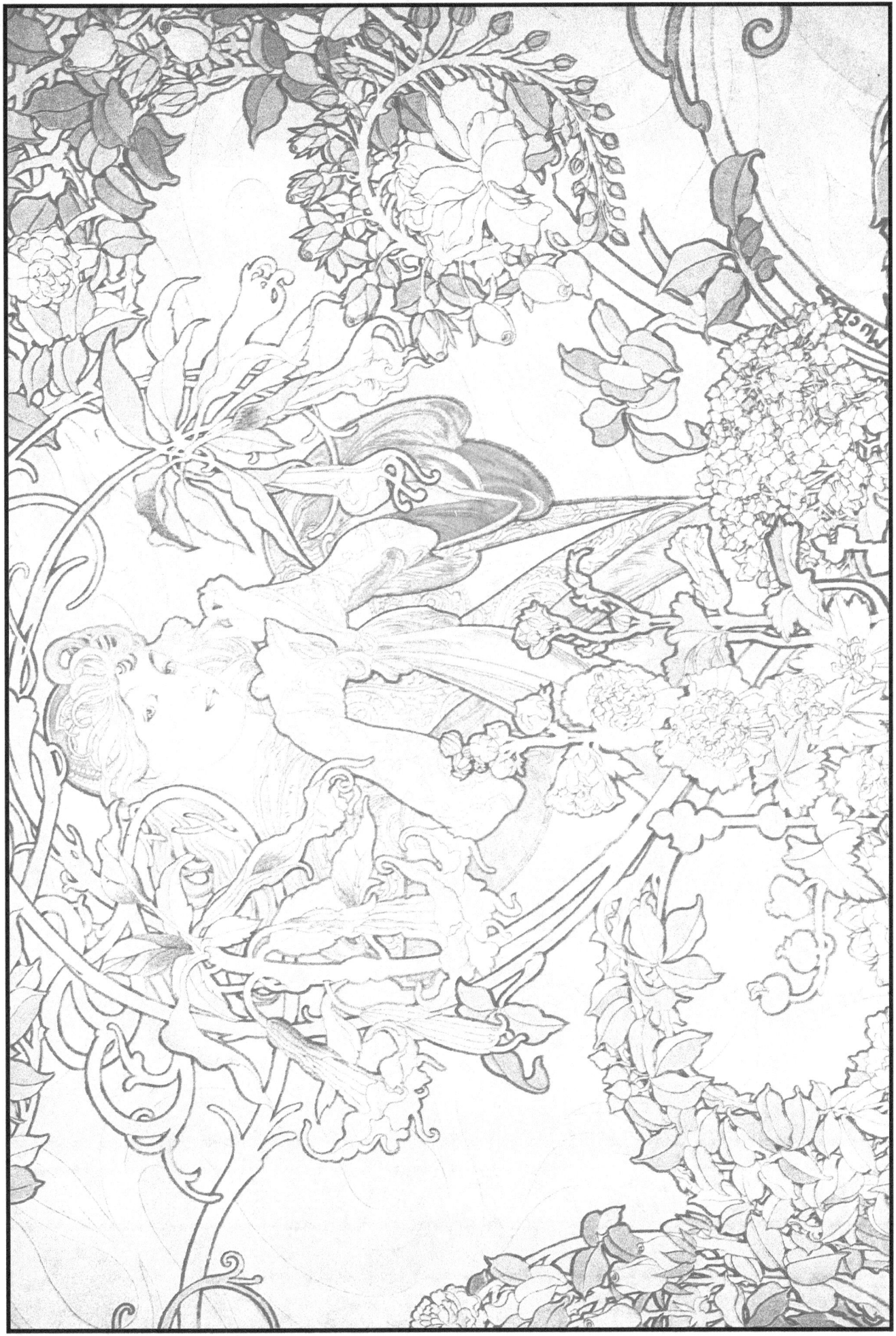

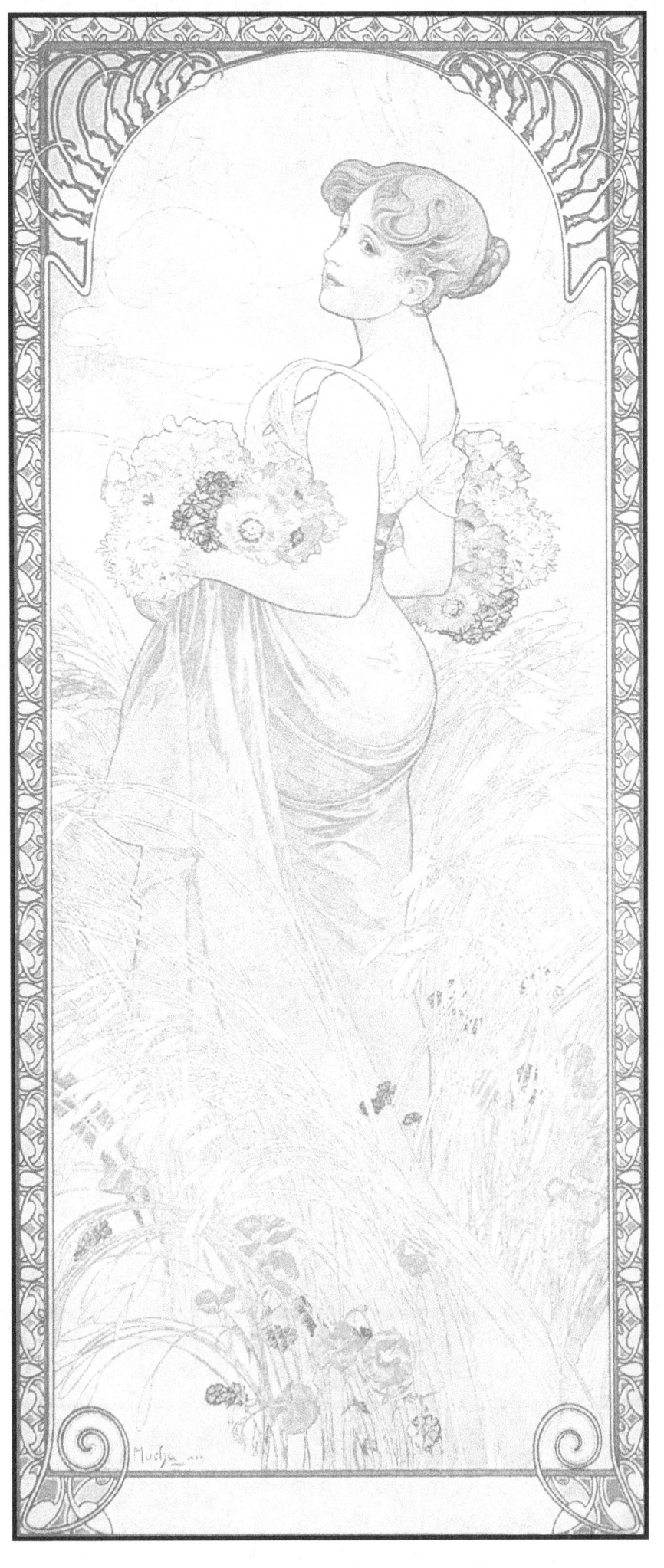

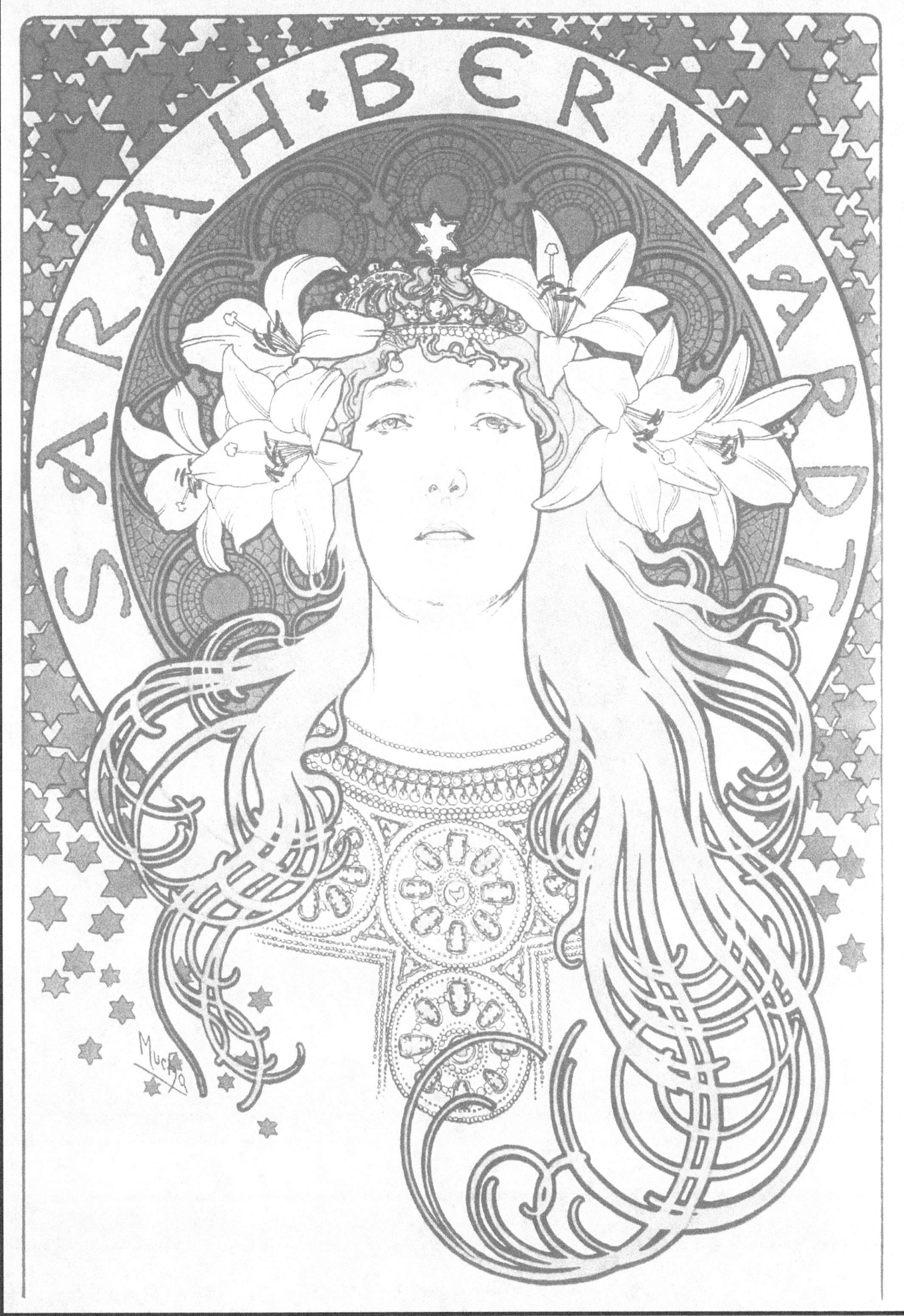

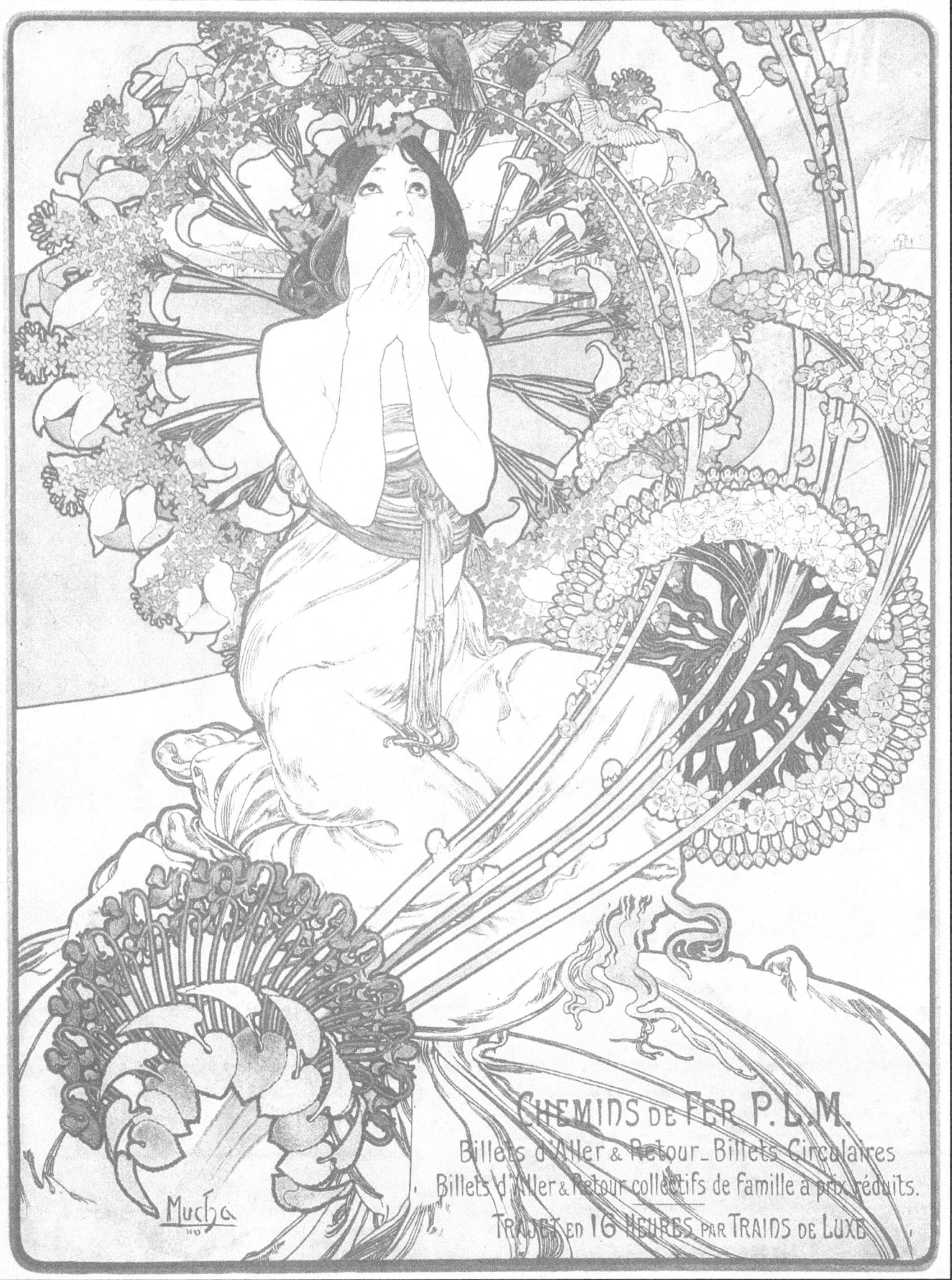

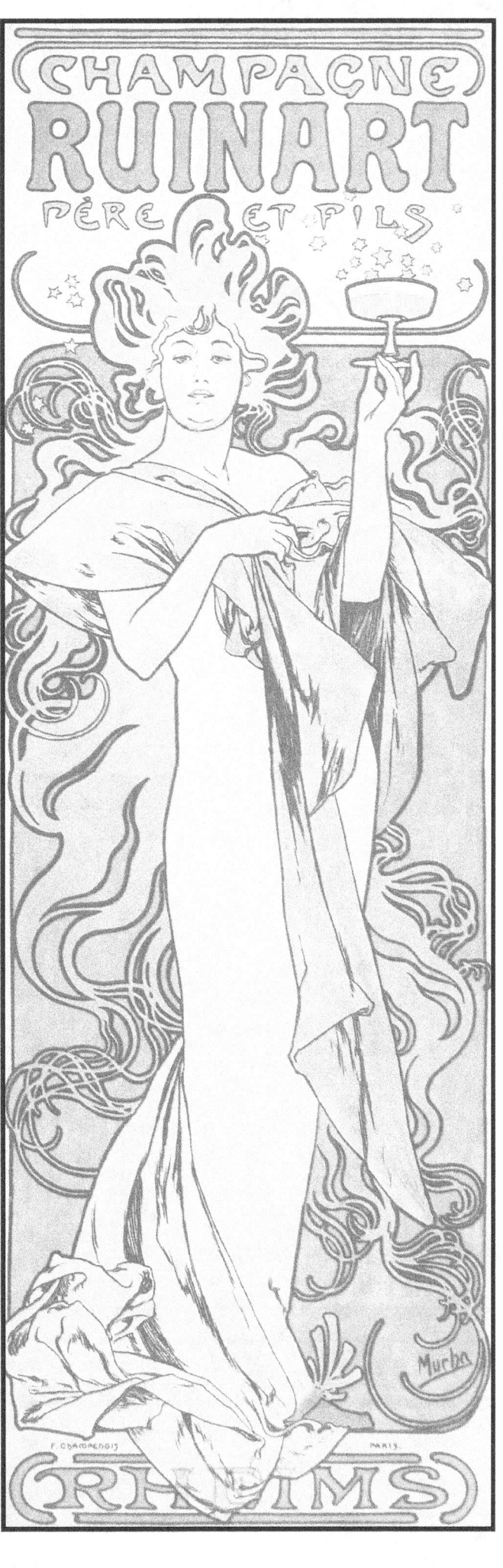

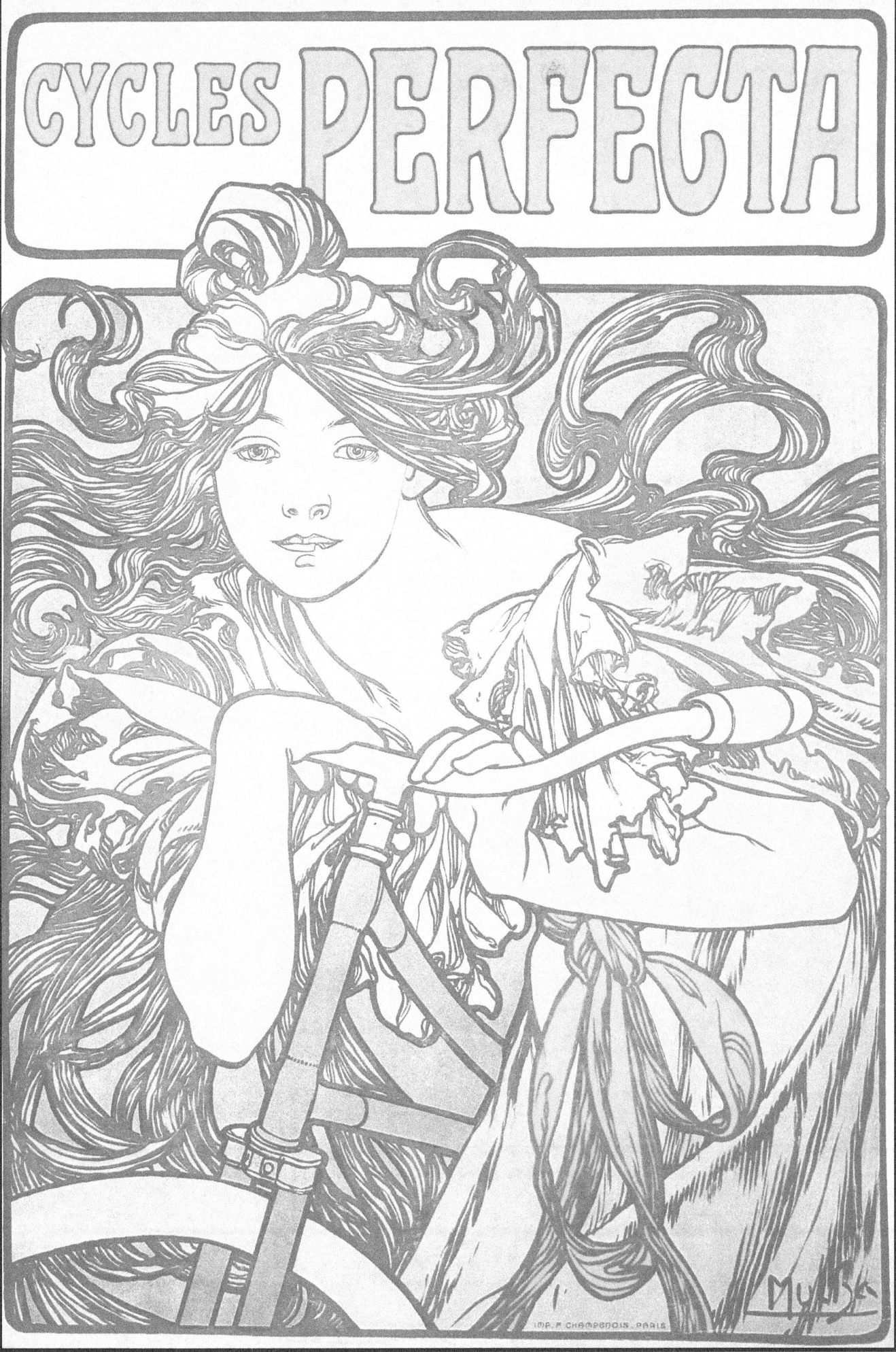

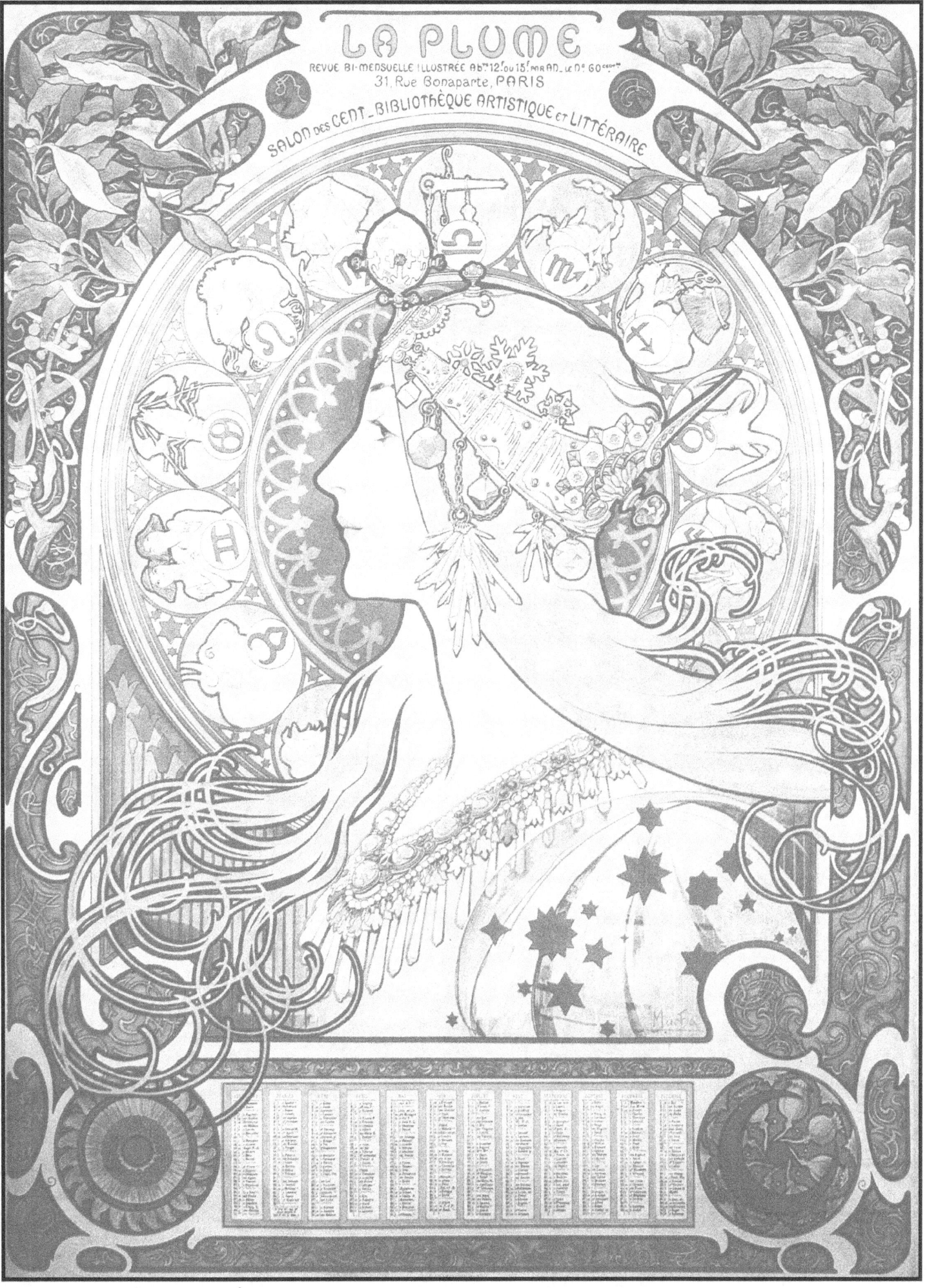

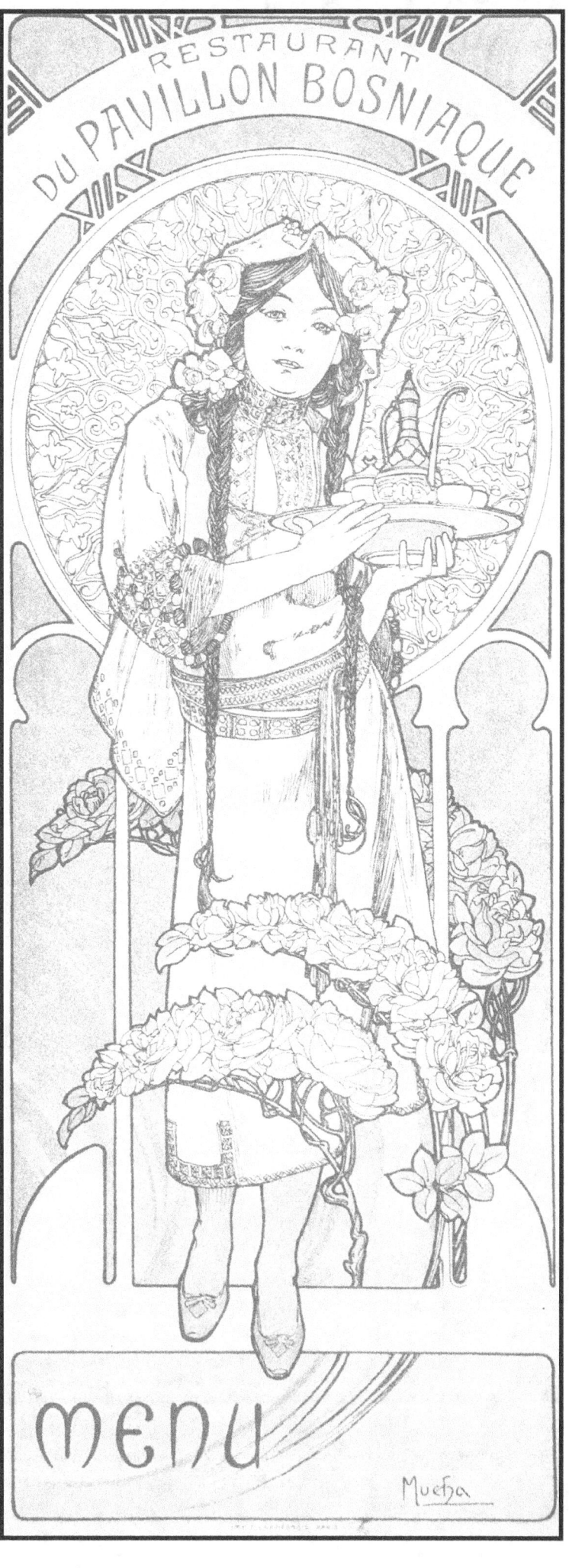